NOTES

P9-CKQ-580

Grammar Guide and contents edited by:
Carol Suplicki B.A.
and
Dee Monostori B.S.

NOTES

Grammar Guide and contents edited by:
Carol Suplicki B.A.
and
Dee Monostori B.S.

NOTES

NOTES

21. Simple Subject and Predicate

The <u>simple subject</u> is the main word or words in the complete subject. It answers the question: "Who or what is being talked about?"
The <u>simple predicate</u> is the main verb or verbs in the complete predicate. It tells something about the subject.

Examples: Fire burns.

The hot fire in the furnace burns many tons of coal during the cold months of the year.

(In both examples, <u>fire</u> is the <u>simple subject</u>. It answers the question "What is being talked about?" The verb <u>burns</u> is the <u>simple predicate</u>. It tells what action the fire is doing.

To find the <u>simple subject</u> in a question, change the question to a statement: Will you be there? You will be there.

21. Simple Subject and Predicate

22. Compound Subject and Compound Predicate

A <u>compound subject</u> has two or more subjects connected by a conjunction. All of the subjects have the same predicate.

A <u>compound predicate</u> has two or more predicates connected by a conjunction. All of the predicates have the same subject.

Examples: The doctor and the nurse treated the patient.
(The <u>compound subject</u> is <u>doctor and nurse.</u>)
The patient will leave the hospital today and return tomorrow.
(The <u>compound predicate</u> is <u>will leave and return.</u>)

22. Compound Subject and Compound Predicate

23. Subject-Verb (Predicate) Agreement

A <u>subject</u> must agree in number and person with its verb.

Verb forms that require careful use are: is, are, was, were; has, have; and the third person present tense of many verbs.
Examples: The baby is asleep. (singular subject, singular verb)
They are asleep. (plural subject, plural verb)

NOTE: <u>Intervening words</u> between the subject and the verb do not affect the number or person of the verb.
<u>They</u>, together with the baby, <u>are asleep</u>. (plural subject)
<u>The baby</u>, with his brothers and sisters, <u>is asleep</u>. (singular subject)

23. Subject-Verb (Predicate) Agreement

24. Subject-Verb (Predicate) Agreement

<u>Compound subjects</u> can be joined by *and* or by *or* or *nor*.

If joined by **and,** two or more nouns are treated as a plural subject.
If joined by *or* by **nor,** the verb agrees in person and number with the subject nearer to it.

Examples: Ann and Betty go to that school. (plural: Ann and Betty))

Either you or he was making noise. (singular: he)

Either he or you were making noise. (plural: you)

Neither Jim nor Al is going. (singular: Al)

Neither she nor the teachers are coming. (plural: teachers)

<u>Indefinite pronouns</u> are either singular or plural depending on meaning.

Examples: each, one, anyone, everyone: usually singular

both, few, many, several: usually plural

24. Subject-Verb (Predicate) Agreement

25. Subject Complement

There are two kinds of *subject complements:*

1. A <u>predicate nominative</u> is a noun or pronoun that follows a linking verb and refers to the subject.
   Example: Jim is the captain. (The noun <u>captain</u> follows the linking verb <u>is</u> and refers to the subject <u>Jim</u>.)
2. A <u>predicate adjective</u> is an adjective that follows a linking verb and describes the subject of the verb.
   Example: The trees are very tall. (The adjective <u>tall</u> follows the linking verb <u>are</u> and describes the subject <u>trees</u>.)

25. Subject Complement

26. Kinds of Sentences

1. A <u>declarative sentence</u> makes a statement. (He is just a baby.)

2. An <u>interrogative sentence</u> asks a question. (Who are his parents?)

3. An <u>imperative sentence</u> gives a command or makes a request.
   You is understood to be the subject of the sentence.
   Do not cross the street when the light is red. (a command)
   Please pass the salt. (a request)

4. An <u>exclamatory sentence</u> expresses strong feeling. I love English!

26. Kinds of Sentences

5. Direct and Indirect Objects of Verbs

A <u>direct object</u> receives the action of the verb and names who or what was acted upon.

Example: He opened the window. (The <u>direct object</u> is window.)

An <u>indirect object</u> is the person or thing to which or for which the action is done. It often comes between the verb and direct object.

Example: Please give me an orange. (The <u>indirect object</u> is me. There is also a <u>direct object</u>, orange.)

5. Direct and Indirect Objects of Verbs

6. Noun

A <u>noun</u> is a word that names a person, place, thing, idea, quality, or action. A proper noun names a particular person, place, or thing. A proper noun always starts with a capital letter.

Examples: Norman   California   Delta Airlines   New York City

A <u>common noun</u> names any one of a class of persons, places, or things.
Examples: state   island   explorer   airline   city   apple

6. Noun

27. Run-on Sentence

A <u>run-on sentence</u> is one in which two sentences are run together without punctuation or by using a comma only. To test for a <u>run-on sentence</u>, find the subjects and predicates.
A <u>run-on sentence</u> is an incorrect sentence construction.

Example: We were hungry after our long hike, we built a fire to cook.
      Correction 1: Use a period to make two sentences.
      Correction 2: Use a comma and a conjunction, such as and.
      Correction 3: Use a semicolon.
      Correction 4: Use a subordinate conjunction, such as
                      because.

27. Run-on Sentence

28. Sentence Fragment

A <u>sentence fragment</u> does not express a complete thought. It is only a piece of a sentence, and it cannot stand alone as a sentence. A <u>sentence fragment</u> is an incorrect sentence construction.

Fragment: The turtle swimming in the pond.
Sentence: The turtle was swimming in the pond.

Fragment: On the beach near the water's edge.
Sentence: We found many shells on the beach near the water's edge.

Fragment: A dictionary to consult
Sentence: The teacher gave me a dictionary to consult.

28. Sentence Fragment

29. Case of Nouns

<u>Case</u> shows relationship of the noun to the rest of a sentence. There are three cases.
1. <u>Nominative case</u> is a noun used as a subject, predicate noun, or direct address, or used as an appositive of one of these.
2. <u>Possessive case</u> is a noun that shows ownership.
3. <u>Objective case</u> is a noun used as a direct or indirect object, subject of an infinitive, object of a preposition, or used as an appositive.

NOTE: An <u>appositive</u> is a noun or pronoun placed after another noun or pronoun to explain or identify. Ms. Brown, my <u>teacher</u>, was there.

29. Case of Nouns

30. Case of Pronouns

The <u>case</u> of a pronoun, also known as a noun equivalent, is determined by the same rules as the case of a noun.

Case of Personal Pronouns

	Singular Nominative	Possessive	Objective
1st person	I	my, mine	me
2nd person	you	your, yours	you
3rd person	he, she, it	his, her, hers, its	him, her, it

Plural

1st person	we	our, ours	us
2nd person	you	your, yours	you
3rd person	they	their, theirs	them

30. Case of Pronouns

31. Clauses

A <u>clause</u> is a group of words containing a subject and a predicate.

An <u>independent clause</u> contains a subject and a predicate and stands alone as a sentence. It is also called a <u>main clause</u>.
Example: Nicole has a cat.
If <u>two independent clauses</u> are connected by a conjunction, they form a <u>compound sentence.</u>
Example: Nicole has a cat, and it sleeps in her room.
A <u>dependent (subordinate) clause</u> cannot stand alone. It needs an independent clause to express a complete thought.
Example: Nicole drew her cat's picture, which is now in the library.

31. Clauses

32. Kinds of Dependent Clauses

A <u>noun clause</u> is a group of words with a subject and a predicate which is used as a noun. It may be used as a subject, a predicate noun, a direct or indirect object, the object of a preposition, or an appositive.

<u>Whichever class you choose</u> is okay. (noun clause used as a subject)
Cooking is <u>what she likes best</u>. (noun clause as a predicate noun)
You know <u>that the teacher is correct</u>. (noun clause as a direct object)

An <u>adjective clause</u> modifies a noun or pronoun. Adjective clauses begin with <u>relative pronouns</u> such as: who, whose, whom, which, what, that.

An <u>adverb clause</u> modifies a verb, an adjective, or another adverb. An adverb clause tells how, when, where, why, to what extent, or under.

32. Kinds of Dependent Clauses

1. Verb

A <u>verb</u> expresses action or a state of being.

<u>Action verbs</u> take direct objects.

Example: Jack <u>hit</u> the <u>ball</u>. <u>Hit</u> is the action. <u>Ball</u> receives the action.

<u>State-of-being verbs</u> link the subject with a noun or pronoun which follows the verb.

Example: John is president. <u>John</u> and <u>president</u> are the same people.

<u>State-of-being verbs</u> also link the subject with an adjective.

Example: <u>Mary</u> is pretty. Mary is the subject. Pretty is the adjective that refers to Mary.

Other sensory or intransitive verbs are as follows.

taste   smell   sound   feel   look   grow   become
appear   seem

1. Verb

2. Verb Phrase

A <u>verb phrase</u> is a main verb plus one or more helping verbs. The helping verb, or verbs, may be separated from the main verb. Helping verbs are also called auxiliary verbs.

Example: He was riding his bike home.
    <u>was riding</u> is the verb phrase; <u>was</u> is the helping verb

The helping verbs are: have, do, shall, will, may, can, must, ought, and any of their derived forms.

Example: be and derived forms: am, is, are, was, were, been, being.

2. Verb Phrase

7. Compound and Collective Nouns

A <u>compound noun</u> is a noun made of two or more words.

Examples:

| ice cream | bookcase | sister-in-law | twenty-two |
| cell-like | lightbulb | extra-large | battlefield |

1. Use a hyphen with a compound word where omission of the hyphen could cause confusion: re-creation (distinct from recreation).

2. Write prefixes and combining forms without hyphens: today; byway; afterthought; antitoxin; semicircle.

A <u>collective noun</u> names a group of people, places, or things of the same kind: group, class, majority, crowd, herd, mob, club, team.

7. Compound and Collective Nouns

8. Noun Gender and Number

The <u>gender</u> of a noun refers to the sex of the person or persons named, or to the inapplicability of sex, as with things, ideas, qualities, or actions. There are three types of gender:

Masculine	man, father, Dr. John Arthur
Feminine:	woman, mother, Dr. Mary Byrd
Neuter:	tree, house, ink, doctor

The <u>number of a noun</u> tells whether the noun names one thing (singular) or more than one thing (plural).

Singular:	boy, girl, movie, insect, guess
Plural:	boys, girls, movies, insects, guesses

8. Noun Gender and Number

9. Pronoun

A <u>pronoun</u> is a word used instead of a noun. It is a substitute for a noun. (The prefix *pro* means for.)

With the exception of indefinite pronouns, a pronoun must agree in person, number, and gender with its <u>antecedent</u>. The <u>antecedent</u> is the noun to which the pronoun refers or for which it stands.

Examples: Mr. Bennett has misplaced his keys.
Mrs. Bennett loaned him her keys.

his, him - Mr. Bennett   her - Mrs. Bennett

9. Pronoun

10. Pronoun Types

1. <u>Personal</u> pronouns refer to the person who is speaking, spoken to, or spoken about.
   Examples: I, me, my, you, your, he, his, she her, hers, they, their, them
2. <u>Interrogative</u> pronouns ask questions.
   Forms: who, whose, whom, which, what
3. <u>Demonstrative</u> pronouns point out something.
   Forms: this, that, these, those, few, many, some, such, all, either.
4. <u>Indefinite</u> pronouns stand for a person, place, or thing that has not been definitely defined. Samples: all, any, both, either, each, many
5. <u>Relative</u> pronouns introduce a subordinate clause and refer to an antecedent.
   Forms: who, whose, whom, which, what, that

10. Pronoun Types

11. Person of Pronouns

The <u>person</u> of a pronoun is defined in three classes:
1. <u>First person</u> indicates that the person is the speaker.
   Examples: I, we, my, mine, our, ours, me, us

2. <u>Second person</u> indicates that the person is the person spoken to.
   Examples: you, your, yours

3. <u>Third person</u> indicates that the person is one spoken about.
   Examples: he, she, it, they, him, her, hers, its, their, theirs, them

Examples: <u>He</u> can't go with <u>you</u> because <u>his</u> sister is sick.
<u>He</u> is third person. <u>You</u> is second person. <u>His</u> is third person.

11. Person of Pronouns

12. Adjective

An <u>adjective</u> describes, limits or modifies a noun or a pronoun.
Adjectives tell what kind, which one, or how many.

Examples: <u>The oldest</u> girl drove <u>a used</u> car.

<u>The four</u> brothers were all <u>good</u> students.

Ken is <u>very tall</u>.

NOTE: The definite article **the** and the indefinite articles **a** and **an** are adjectives.

A <u>proper adjective</u> is a proper noun either used as an adjective or made from a proper noun. It describes a noun or pronoun, and it always begins with a capital letter.

Examples: The <u>Spanish</u> teacher is from Madrid.

The ambitious politician struck a <u>Lincolnesque</u> pose.

Shakespeare lived during <u>Elizabethan</u> times.

12. Adjective

13. Adverb

Definition: An adverb modifies a verb, an adjective, or another adverb.
It may tell how, when, where, to what extent, how much, or why.
Many adverbs are made by adding **ly** to an adjective.
NOTE: The word *not* is always an adverb.

Making adverbs by adding ly to adjectives		Examples of adverbs that do not end in ly	
rapid	rapidly	when	soon
calm	calmly	where	far
quick	quickly	why	too
sad	sadly	then	always
strange	strangely	now	very
cheerful	cheerfully	never	late

13. Adverb

14. Preposition

A <u>preposition</u> is a linking word that shows the relationship between a noun or pronoun and some other word in a sentence. A preposition usually starts a phrase.

Examples: until; tomorrow; on the way; to him.

These sample prepositions indicate:

position	in, on, under, with, among
direction	from, to, into, up, down, through
time	about, at, before, after
cause	because of, for, since
possession	of

14. Preposition

15. Prepositional Phrases

A <u>prepositional phrase</u> is a group of words that begins with a preposition and includes a noun or pronoun. The noun or pronoun in the phrase is called the object of the preposition. There are two kinds:

1. An <u>adjective phrase</u> modifies or alters the meaning of a noun or pronoun.
   Example: The singers from Italy will perform. (The adjective phrase <u>from Italy</u> modifies the subject <u>singers</u>.)
2. An <u>adverb phrase</u> modifies a verb, an adjective, or another adverb.
   Example: The singers from Italy will perform at Symphony Hall. (The adverb phrase <u>at Symphony Hall</u> modifies the verb <u>will perform.</u>)

15. Prepositional Phrases

16. Conjunction

A conjunction is a linking word that connects or joins words, phrases, clauses, or sentences.

<u>Coordinate conjunctions</u> (and, but, or, nor, for) are used to connect words, phrases, clauses, or sentences of equal rank.

<u>Subordinate conjunctions</u> link a subordinate clause to a main clause in a sentence.

Examples: after, because, until, as, as if, whether, where, when, since

Some subordinate conjunctions are also used as prepositions, as: after, before, since, until.

<u>Correlative conjunctions</u> are used in pairs: both-and, either-or.

16. Conjunction

17. Interjection

An <u>interjection</u> is an exclamatory word which has no direct relationship to any other word in the sentence but modifies the sentence as a whole.

Examples:
   Ouch!   Oh!   Yes!   Hey!   Yeah!   Wow!

Examples:
   Yes! Tom passed all his classes.
   Hey! Watch where you're going.
   She shouted, "Oh! I got an A!"

17. Interjection

18. Sentence

A <u>sentence</u> is a group of words expressing a complete thought or several thoughts so closely related that they constitute a thought unit.

Every sentence must have a subject and a predicate.

Jane mailed a letter.

Jane wrote a letter, went to the post office, and mailed it.

When you're ready, call me and I'll meet you at the store.

18. Sentence

19. Subject

A sentence must have a <u>subject</u> and a predicate.

The <u>subject</u> of a sentence is a noun or noun equivalent together with all its modifiers, about which something is said.

Examples: My sister made a cake. (<u>My sister</u> is the complete subject.)
The little white kitten lapped up the milk. (<u>The little white kitten</u> is the complete subject.)

The <u>simple subject</u> is the main word or words: sister, kitten.

19. Subject

20. Predicate

A sentence must have a subject and a <u>predicate</u>.

The <u>predicate</u> of a sentence is a verb, together with all its modifiers, that defines the action of state or the subject.

Examples: The orchestra played marches. (The complete predicate is <u>played marches</u>.)
We often go to the library after school. (The complete predicate is <u>go to the library after school.</u>)

The complete predicate is the main verb with its modifiers.
The simple predicate is the main verb: played, go.

20. Predicate

1. Apostrophe in contractions and plurals

An apostrophe is used to replace letters omitted in contractions.

he is	he's	were not	weren't	she will	she'll
do not	don't	would not	wouldn't	you are	you're
it is	it's	do not	don't	they will	they'll

An apostrophe is used to form the plural of numbers, letters, or words referred to as words.

Examples: In the decimal system, we count by 10's.
Watch your p's and q's.
Avoid using too many very's in your writing.

1. Apostrophe in contractions and plurals

2. Apostrophe with possessive nouns

Add an apostrophe and **s** to form the possessive case of nouns which do not end in **s**.

Jack's car	lady's dress	somebody's book
men's shoes	women's dresses	children's party

Add an apostrophe alone to form the possessive case of nouns which end in **s**.

Owens' car   ladies' dresses   players' gloves

2. Apostrophe with possessive nouns

3. Apostrophe in possessive word groups

Use an apostrophe to show possession in word groups.

<u>Compound Words</u> - Add an apostrophe and s to the last word.
mother-in-law's hat   passer-by's car

<u>Joint Ownership</u> - Use an apostrophe in the name just before the object possessed.

Nicole and Cara's school project (one project)

<u>Individual Ownership</u> - Use an apostrophe in each name.
Benjamin's and Jane's book reports (two reports)

3. Apostrophe in possessive word groups

4. Capitalization in sentences and poetry

Capitalize the first word in a sentence or, often, in a line of poetry.

    The book is in the library.   Max has the book.

In poetry, it is conventional to capitalize the first word of each line.

> When writing poetry you use rhyme,
> Plus a smattering of punctuation,
> And for every line, every time,
> The first word requires capitalization.

Some poets exercise "poetic license" and ignore this rule
(for example, e. e. cummings wrote his poetry without any capitals).

4. Capitalization in sentences and poetry

5. Capitalization in direct quotations

"Are you going to Mary's party?" Jane asked.
"Yes," replied Wendy, "but I don't know what to wear."

Notice that **but** in Wendy's answer is not capitalized because the entire quotation is one sentence.

"We should leave early," Wendy said. "Traffic might be heavy."

Notice that **Traffic** is capitalized because the quoted words are two sentences.

5. Capitalization in direct quotations

6. Capitalization with names, titles, and proper adjectives

Names of persons: Abraham Lincoln   Mary Todd

Capitalize proper adjectives formed from proper nouns:
  Asian flu   English history   Senator Cole

Titles are capitalized when used in place of a name:
  Will your men be in the parade, Sergeant?

Capitalize initials and title abbreviations:
  Dr. L. A. Johnson   Noah Smith, Jr.   Sgt. Blake

6. Capitalization with names, titles, and proper adjectives

7. Capitalization with relationships, religions, nationalities, etc.

Capitalize family relationship words used alone as names.
> Will Mom be home soon, Dad?
> They visited Uncle Bill in Washington, D.C.

Capitalize names of religions, nationalities, races, languages, and proper adjectives based on them:

Protestant   Spanish   Catholic   Jewish   Indian

> We studied the Jewish religion.
> The Spanish language is spoken in many countries of
> South America as well as in Spain.

7. Capitalization with relationships, religions, nationalities, etc.

8. Capitalization with months, days, and geographic names

Capitalize months of the year and days of the week.

January   June   Monday   Tuesday

The names of the seasons are not capitalized.

spring   summer   fall (autumn) winter

Capitalize geographical names.

Pacific Ocean   Gulf of Mexico   North America
Whittle Avenue   Central Park   Grand Canyon

Capitalize compass points when they refer to location, **not** to direction.

8. Capitalization with months, days, and geographical names

9. Capitalization with organizational names

Capitalize the names of organizations and subjects.

Central High School	Antique Automobile Association
New York Symphony	Department of Labor

Capitalize the names of school subjects that come from names of countries or languages.

Latin	English	South American History	French

Capitalize the names of other school subjects only when referring to a specific course in a general area.

She is in the Algebra 1 class. (specific course of study)

She is studying algebra. (general area of study)

9. Capitalization with organizational names

10. Capitalization with titles

Capitalize titles of written works, art works, musical works, etc.
Capitalize *a, an,* or *the* only when it is the first word of a title:
<u>The Call of the Wild</u>   "A Christmas Carol "

Conjunctions and prepositions (except ones that are four or more letters long) are not capitalized in titles.
<u>Pride and Prejudice</u>   <u>Drums Along the Mohawk</u>

Capitalize titles of holidays and special events, historical periods, famous documents, and notable constructions: Memorial Day   Homecoming
Stone Age   Magna Carta   Empire State Building   Air Force One

10. Capitalization with titles

11. Colon

Use a colon to introduce a list or series.
   The students were asked to bring the following items to school: pens, pencils, erasers, and papers.

Use a colon in writing the salutation of a business letter.
   Dear Sir: Dear Mr. Banks: Dear Dr. Jones: Gentlemen:

Use a colon in numerals that indicate time.
   3:45 p.m.   12:00 noon

Use a colon to indicate volume and page numbers: AMA Journal 5:21

11. Colon

12. Commas with addresses and dates

Commas are used after the parts of addresses.
The grocery store is located at 1121 Western Avenue, Lansing, KS.

The class wrote get well cards to Martha at her home address, 333 Elm Street, Apartment B3, New York City, NY 10001.

Commas are used to set off the year in a date.
He graduated in June, 1991.
The state fair was held from May 1, 1997 to May 5, 1997.
Where were you on September 5, 1998?

The comma is sometimes omitted between the name of the month and the year if the day is not given: November 1962   June 1991

12. Commas with addresses and dates

13. Commas with person addressed and mild exclamations

Commas are used to set off a name of direct address.
Let me introduce my new teacher to you, Ms. Wright.
Yes, young man, the bus to the stadium stops here.
Where are you going, Henry?

A comma is used with an expression that is a mild exclamation, requiring some mark of punctuation to represent a break in thought but not so strong a mark as the exclamation or period.
Yes, I've completed the biology program.
No, they can't go to the movies tonight.
Oh, aren't you John's brother?
Well, we'll have to find another way to get to the game.

13. Commas with person addressed and mild exclamations

14. Commas in a series

Word series:
She is studying English, civics, mathematics, and physics.

Number series:
Little Joe likes to count his fingers by twos: counting 2, 4, 6, 8, and 10.

Phrase series:
The parade was watched at the school, at the library, and at the park.

Clause series:
The editor reads a story, makes corrections, and returns it to the writer.

14. Commas in a series

They thought it was too expensive, also.
(The first *too* is an adjective; it is not used to mean *also*.)
Both March and April were unusually cool that year.

A comma is used when a short clause changes a statement into an interrogative or exclamatory sentence.
You were in school today, weren't you? Believe me, I was!

A comma is used to avoid misunderstanding.
After the audience left, the room was closed.

15. Commas to make the meaning of a sentence clear

16. Commas with parenthetical and appositive expressions

Commas are used to set off <u>parenthetical expressions</u>, *which* are word groups that are not necessary to the meaning of a sentence.

A person's home, surprisingly, has the highest accident rate.

Improper use of ladders, for example, may result in falls.

Household cleaners, such as bleach, are dangerous if swallowed.

<u>Appositive expressions</u> are word groups that explain a word that they follow.

The diamond, a very hard crystalline of carbon, is used in industry and as a gem in jewelry.

Delaware, the first state, is located on the Atlantic coast.

Mr. James, a lawyer and a well-known writer, is running for mayor.

16. Commas with parenthetical and appositive expressions

17. Commas with non-restrictive clauses and phrases

<u>Non-restrictive clauses and phrases</u> are word groups that are **not** necessary to the meaning of a sentence.

The roof, which is twenty years old, has started to leak.

Mr. Davis, standing in the doorway, is my teacher.

(Test the sentence for meaning by removing the clause or phrase.)

Commas are **not** used around restrictive clauses and phrases that **are** necessary to the meaning of a sentence.

A roof that leaks needs immediate repair.

The man standing in the doorway is my teacher.

17. Commas with non-restrictive clauses and phrases

18. Commas with word groups used as introductions

A comma sets off introductory word groups.

Introductory clause:
As they walked away, we waved goodbye.

Participial phrase:
Having completed our homework, we played games.

Prepositional phrase:
During the school year, children go to bed early.

18. Commas with word groups used as introductions

19. Commas with *and, but, or, nor, for*

A compound sentence is one that is made up of two sentences joined by *and, but, or, nor,* as well as the word *for*. Use a comma after the first sentence.

My bicycle has a flat tire, and I don't know how to fix it.

I can't fix it, but my brother can do it.

We will have to leave now, Bob, or we will be late.

He couldn't climb the tree, nor could he coax the cat to come down.

19. Commas with *and, but, or, nor, for*

20. Commas and capitalization in formatting letters

A comma is used after the beginning and the closing expressions used in writing a friendly letter and after the closing expressions in writing a business letter. Capitalize only the first word in the closing of a letter.

Dear Grace,	Dear Ken and Nancy,	Dear Mom,
Sincerely yours,	Your friend,	Very truly yours,
With love,	Best regards,	Regards,

Capitalization of the first word and all <u>nouns</u> in the salutation of a letter applies to both formal and informal letters:

Dear Sir: Dear Nancy,   My dear Aunt and Uncle,

20. Commas and capitalization in formatting letters

21. Dashes and Parentheses

The dash is about twice the length of the hyphen.
Use a dash to indicate a change in thought or a parenthetical idea.

> If Joe had only caught that fly ball – but we won the game anyway.
> That movie– have you seen it? – is too scary for children.

Use parentheses to enclose words, phrases, or sentences that offer explanation without changing the meaning of the statement.

> Some plants (cactus, for example) can survive with little water.
> John Milton (1608 –1674) was both a poet and a government official.
> I enclose a check for five dollars ($5.00).

Instead of parentheses within parentheses, use brackets.

> The next reading is in <u>Macbeth</u> (IV, i, 25 ff. [p.41]).

21. Dashes and Parentheses

22. Sentence End Punctuation

A **period** ends a sentence that states a fact (declarative) or gives a command (imperative).

Declarative Example: The swimmer practiced every day.

Imperative Example: Do warm-up exercises before you swim.

A **question mark** ends a sentence that asks a question (interrogative).
Interrogative Example: When will the swimming meet be held?

An **exclamation point** ends a sentence that expresses strong feeling or surprise.
Exclamatory Example: Be careful!

22. Sentence End Punctuation

23. Hyphen

Hyphens are used to divide words and to form compound words.
Use hyphens to divide words between syllables at the end of a line:

pre-vent   know-ledge   cook-ing

Words of one syllable should not be divided.

popped   not pop-ped

Divide words with double consonants between the double
consonants: rat-tle, mid-dle

Use hyphens with fractions used as adjectives: one-half teaspoon
Use hyphens with compound numbers: twenty-two or thirty-three
Use hyphens with compound titles: president-elect
Use hyphens with compound adjectives when they precede the word
they modify: fifth-floor apartment

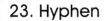

23. Hyphen

24. Periods in abbreviations

Periods are used with initials, personal titles, in addresses, in dates, in time and date notation, and in many shortened versions of words.

Examples: Dr. West   Ms. Jane Wise   Mr. R. Abbott, Sr.   Main St.   P.O.

Mon.   Dec.   4:30 p.m.   A. D.   1776   abbr.   c.o.d.

Abbreviations used in footnotes: ed. (edition) Vol. (Volume) Chap.

(Chapter)   p., pp. (page, pages) f., ff. (page, pages following)

Some abbreviations do **not** use periods:

Post Office-approved abbreviations for states do not end with periods:

AK DC MD NC ND NJ NY PA RI SC SD WV

Standard country abbreviations do **not** use periods: FIN, MEX, USA

Metric system abbreviations do **not** use periods:

m meter   g gram   cm centimeter

24. Periods in abbreviations

25. Periods used in outlines

In outlines use periods after numbers and letters. Periods are not used with numbers or letters that are enclosed in parentheses.

    1. Topic...
      A. Topic...
      B. Topic...
        1. Topic...
        2. Topic...
          a. Topic...
          b. Topic...
            (1) Topic...
            (2) Topic...
    2. Topic...

25. Periods used in outlines

26. Quotation marks and commas with direct quotations

Quotation marks are used to enclosed direct quotations. Direct quotations contain the exact words spoken by the person or reference being quoted. Commas are placed inside of closing quotation marks.
    "Your dress will be ready tomorrow," the cleaner promised.
    "I'm on my way to the station and can't stop," said Fran.

Do **not** use quotation marks around indirect quotations.
    Fran said that she was on her way to the station and couldn't stop.

If the quoted words require a question mark or an exclamation point, put it inside the closing quotation mark. "Will you write to me?" she asked.

26. Quotation marks and commas with direct quotations

27. Single quotations marks in nested quotations

Quotation mark symbols are ' (single) and " (double).
<u>Nested quotations</u> are quotations within quotations. Double and single quotation marks are alternated as many times as needed to complete the quotation sequence.

He said, "Wes asked Rob, 'Will you give me a ride home?' "

The doctor explained to the mother, "Your child told me, 'Doctor, my mother said "Don't climb the tree" but I didn't listen. I did climb the tree and I did fall.' "

27. Single quotation marks in nested quotations

28. Quotation marks with periods and commas

"We'll be there soon," she said. "Please wait for us."

I read the poem "Trees" to the class. Joyce Kilmer wrote "Trees."

The teacher quoted the line from Lincoln's "Gettysburg Address": "...that government of the people, by the people, and for the people shall not perish from the earth."

The coach said, "I hope you'll be on the team"; then he added, "we're having tryouts Saturday."

28. Quotation marks with periods and commas

29. Quotation marks with ? and ! marks

<u>Quotation marks are placed *outside*</u> of a question mark or an exclamation mark if that punctuation mark is part of the quotation.

He asked, "Who was the greatest president of the United States?"

They shouted, "Go, team!"

<u>Quotation marks are placed inside</u> of a ? or an ! if that punctuation is **not** part of the quotation.
Did he say "I won't go to school"?

29. Quotation marks with ? and ! marks

30. Quotation marks with titles

Quotation marks are used with: titles of articles, chapters, short stories, or art works; titles of short plays, poems, or musical compositions; and titles of radio, television, or video programs.

> She bought a print of Van Gogh's painting "Starry Night."
> "Richard Cory" is a poem with a message.

Use an underline with these items: titles of books, long plays, musical compositions, or films; titles of magazines and newspapers; names of aircraft, spacecraft, ships, and trains.

> There was a review of the <u>Titanic</u> movie in <u>Time</u> magazine.
> The <u>USS Arizona</u> ship is a memorial to those lost at sea.

30. Quotation marks with titles

31. Semicolons with commas in a series

Semicolons are used between the items in a series if the items themselves contain commas.

Club officers are Beth Jones, president; Cal Smith, vice president; Art Day, secretary; and Ruth Allen, treasurer.

Representatives at the convention came from Dearborn, Michigan; Miami, Florida; and Sacramento, California.

31. Semicolons with commas in a series

32. Semicolon with conjunctive adverbs

A semicolon is used before a conjunctive adverb that connects two clauses or by itself between two parts of a compound sentence.

Some common conjunctive adverbs are:

however	moreover	consequently	furthermore
besides	therefore	hence	so
still	yet	otherwise	also
thus	instead	nevertheless	

Examples: Traffic laws can be irritating; however, they save lives.
We were hot; we ate ice cream cones.

32. Semicolons with conjunctive adverbs

NOTES

PHONICS

NOTES

1. Vowels and Consonants

A vowel is one of the following letters: **a**, **e**, **i**, **o**, **u** and sometimes **y**.

The letter **y** is considered a vowel when it has the sound of either **i** or **e**.

A consonant is any of the other letters of the alphabet.

A digraph is two letters that blend together to form one sound.

The **ea** in meat is a vowel digraph.

The **sh** in shoe is a consonant digraph.

1. Vowels and Consonants

2. Syllables and Words

Words are made up of parts called **syllables**.
Each syllable has one vowel sound.

A word with one vowel sound has one syllable.
Examples: ink, stand, blue, disk, scream

A word with two vowel sounds has two syllables.
Examples: believe, handsome, action, throughout

Some words have more than two syllables.

three syllables:	different, syllables
four syllables:	differently, scientific
five syllables:	syllabication, examination

2. Syllables and Words

The ă vowel sound is the sound you hear in the middle of **can**.
The ă vowel sound is most often spelled **a**.
Examples: hand   branch   ragged   add   after   plant
Sometimes two letters can make the ă vowel sound.
Examples: plaid   laugh

The ĕ vowel sound is the sound you hear in the middle of **bed**.
The ĕ vowel sound is most often spelled as **e**.
Examples: tent   trench   red   welcome   end   tense
Sometimes the letters **ea** together make the ĕ sound.
Examples: bread   together   weather   breath

3. Short Vowel ă and ĕ

4. Short Vowel ĭ and ŏ

The ĭ vowel sound is the sound you hear in the middle of **fix**.
The ĭ vowel sound is most often spelled as i.

Examples:
lift   six   dim   visit   rip   tulip

The ŏ vowel sound is the sound you hear in the middle of **stop**.
The ŏ vowel sound is most often spelled as **o**.

Examples:
shock   promise   proper   common   crop   hop

4. Short Vowel ĭ and ŏ

5. Short Vowel ŭ

The ŭ vowel sound is the sound you hear in the middle of **cup**.

The ŭ vowel sound is most often spelled as u.

Examples of the ŭ vowel sound.

puppy   study   hunger   hungry   fun   plum

5. Short Vowel ŭ

6. Long Vowel ā

The ā vowel sound is the sound you hear in the middle of **bake**.

The ā vowel sound can be spelled in many ways.

Spelling	Examples			
a	paste	ranger	cake	face
ai	stain	brain	gait	bait
ea	steak	great	break	
ei	reindeer	feign	vein	

6. Long Vowel ā

7. Long Vowel ē

The ē vowel sound is the sound you hear at the beginning of **ego**.

The ē vowel sound can be spelled in many ways.

Spelling	Examples	
e	be	he
ee	eel	green
ei	receipt	ceiling
ie	piece	believe
ea	peace	cream
y	eighty	drafty

7. Long Vowel ē

8. Long Vowel ī

The ī vowel sound is the sound you hear in the middle of **bite**.

The ī vowel sound can be spelled in many ways.

Spelling	Examples	
i	kite	slide
ai, ei	aisle	height
igh	delight	right
ui	guide	beguile
uy	buy	guy
y	dry	style

8. Long Vowel ī

9. Long Vowel ō

The ō vowel sound is the sound you hear in the middle of **home**.

The ō vowel sound can be spelled in many ways.

Spelling	Examples	
o	open	clover
	com	prose
oa	float	soap
ou	shoulder	although
ow	own	bellow

9. Long Vowel ō

10. Long Vowel ū

The ū vowel sound is the sound you hear in middle of **cube**.

The ū vowel sound is most often spelled as u.
Examples:

music	cuticle	fume	confuse
usual	acute	amuse	use

Sometimes two or more letters together form the ū vowel sound.

fuel	view	beautiful	cue
few	preview	value	

10. Long Vowel ū

11. Vowel Sound ü

The **ü** vowel sound is the sound you hear in the middle of **soon**.

The **ü** vowel sound can be spelled in many different ways.

Spelling	Examples		
u	flute	truth	blue
	June	tuba	glue
ui	juice	fruit	suit
ew	dew	new	knew
o	do	who	to
oo	spoon	noon	moon
ou	youth	soup	route

11. Vowel Sound ü

12. Vowel Sound û

The û vowel sound is the sound you hear in the middle of **fur.**

The û vowel sound can be spelled in many different ways.

Spelling	Examples			
ur	burn	occur	current	turkey
or	worth	worm	worry	world
our	adjourn	journal	courtesy	journey
er	inert	certain	version	merchant
ir	birthday	circle	thirteen	circus

13. Vowel Sound ôr

The **ôr** sound is the sound you hear in the middle of **horse**.

The **ôr** sound can be spelled in many different ways.

Spelling	Examples		
or	or	normal	torch
	score	fort	implore
oor	door	poor	floor
our	four	court	pour
oar	board	hoard	roar

14. Vowel Sounds âr and är

The âr sound is the sound you hear in the middle of **care**.
The âr sound is usually spelled in these ways.

Spelling	Examples		
ar	dare	flare	rare
air	pair	hair	air
ear	bear	wear	pear

The är sound is the sound you hear in the middle of **hard**.

Examples: card, barn, star, start.

14. Vowel Sounds âr and är

15. Vowel Sounds ou and oi

The **ou** vowel sound is the sound you hear in the middle of **sound**.

The **ou** vowel sound can be spelled **ou** or **ow**.

Spelling	Examples			
ou	hour	thousand	about	gout
ow	clown	allow	power	tower

The **oi** sound is the sound you hear at the end of **boy**.
The sound is spelled **oi** or **oy**.

Spelling	Examples			
oi	voice	moist	point	joint
oy	destroy	loyal	coy	toy

15. Vowel Sounds ou and oi

16. Vowel Sounds əl and ən

The **əl** vowel sound is the sound you hear at the end of **huddle.**
The **əl** vowel sound can be spelled in many different ways.

Spelling	Examples			
le	middle	title	cable	muddle
al	animal	signal	petal	metal
el	camel	label	model	jewel

The **ən** vowel sound is the sound you hear at the end of **even.**
The **ən** vowel sound is usually spelled in these ways.

Spelling	Examples			
en	dozen	listen	spoken	token
in	cousin	bobbin	robin	cabin

16. Vowel Sounds əl and ən

The **ər** vowel sound is the sound you hear in the middle of **germ.**

The **ər** vowel sound can be spelled in different ways.

Spelling	Examples			
ar	polar	popular	jugular	regular
er	term	reverse	merchant	jerk
ir	thirsty	shirk	girth	birthday
or	word	worth	worst	worker
ur	flurry	blur	curve	turkey
ear	research	earth	rehearse	dearth

17. Vowel Sound ər

18. Consonant f

The **f** sound is the sound you hear at the beginning of **far**.

The **f** sound at the beginning of a word is spelled **f**.
Examples of the **f** consonant:

fun	faint	first	fiction	final

The **f** sound at the beginning, middle or end of a word can be spelled as **ph** or **gh**.

Examples of the **ph** or **gh** consonants:

elephant	phone	phantom	nephew	phonics
laugh	enough	cough	tough	rough

18. Consonant f

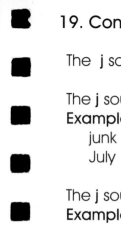

19. Consonant j

The j sound is the sound you hear at the beginning of **jam.**

The j sound at the beginning of a word is spelled j.
Examples of the j consonant:

| junk | justice | jut | June |
| July | jest | jewel | jar |

The j sound at the end of a word can be spelled **ge** or **dge.**
Examples of the **ge** or **dge** spellings:

| average | gauge | beverage | hinge |
| ledge | judge | bridge | edge |

19. Consonant j

20. Consonant k

The **k** sound is the sound you hear at the beginning and end of **kick**.
The **k** sound can be spelled **k, c, ck**.
The letter c usually makes the k sound when it is followed by a or u.
Examples of the **k** consonant sound:

| kind | keep | car | cut | block |

The **kw** sound is spelled **qu**. **Note:** u always follows q in English words.

| quack | quiet | quick | quarrel | queen |

The **ks** sound is spelled **x**.

| next | fix | boxer | text | vex |

20. Consonant k

21. Consonant n

The **n** sound is the sound you hear at the beginning of **not**.

The **n** sound can be spelled in different ways, but **n** is most common.

Spelling	Examples			
n	nap	kind	tent	taint
	navy	prevent	native	note
nn	dinner	beginner	planning	banner
gn	gnu	design	foreign	reign
kn	knee	known	knock	knit

21. Consonant n

22. Consonant s

The **s** sound is the sound you hear at the end of **class**.
The **s** sound is usually spelled **s, ss, c**. It can also be spelled **sc, ce**.
The letter c usually makes the s sound when it is followed by e, I, or y.

Spelling	Examples		
s	sand	sentence	sour
ss	message	less	confess
c	center	cycle	city
sc	science	scissors	miscellaneous
ce	since	sincere	hence

22. Consonant s

23. Digraphs sh, ch, th, wh

Sh, th, wh, are consonant digraphs, which stand together as one sound.

Digraphs		Examples		
sh	shy	shade	should	ashore
	dish	shower	cash	short
ch	chip	church	chill	chocolate
	peach	rich	ranch	leeches
th	thin	father	both	then
	thick	nothing	bother	tenth
wh	whip	when	what	where
	whole	whim	whisk	while

23. Digraphs sh, ch, th, wh

24. Sounds ch and sh

The **ch** sound is the sound you hear at the beginning and end of **church**. It is spelled **ch or tch**.

Spelling	Examples			
ch	chapter	china	charge	teacher
	branch	clench	reach	preach
tch	batch	pitcher	watch	hatch
	match	satchel	sketch	latch

The **sh** sound is the sound you hear at the beginning of **shop**. It is spelled **sh, ch, or s**.

Spelling	Examples			
sh	shake	ship	hush	fish
ch	chevron	chef	parachute	
s	sugar	sure	insure	censure

24. Sounds ch and sh

25. Sounds tion and sion

The letters **tion** and **sion** can sound like **shun**.

Spelling	Examples					
tion	edition	motion	emotion	action	addition	devotion
sion	mission	lesion	passion	version	decision	explosion

25. Sounds tion and sion

26. Blends st, tw, bl

A **blend** is a special sound that is formed when two or three consonants are used together. The sounds are blended together in the word.

Blend	Examples			
st	stay	steam	stamp	state
	stove	stop	stew	start
tw	twine	twist	twelve	twitter
	between	twice	twirl	twin
bl	block	black	blood	blanket
	bland	blue	blizzard	blink

26. Blends st, tw, bl

27. r Blends

Various consonants blend with r.

Blend	Examples			
br	brat	brush	bring	broken
cr	crest	crab	crease	creep
dr	draw	drape	drip	droop
fr	frame	fruit	freak	free
gr	grand	great	green	gripe
pr	prank	preen	price	prone
tr	trunk	track	trip	tree

27. r Blends

28. s Blends

Various consonants blend with s.

Blend		Examples		
sc	scare	scallion	scope	scandal
sk	sky	skull	basket	mask
sl	slip	sly	slope	slush
sm	smile	smoke	smash	smell
sn	snow	snake	snout	snap
sp	spy	spell	wasp	lisp
st	step	star	mast	first
sw	swat	swing	swell	sweater

28. s Blends

29. Blends spr, scr, str, spl, squ

Three letter blends of **spr, scr, str, spl and squ** form many words.

Blend		Examples		
spr	spring	spry	spread	sprocket
scr	scream	screw	scratch	script
str	string	stray	strength	strong
spl	splash	splendor	splice	splotch
squ	squall	squirrel	squiggle	squash

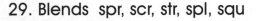

29. Blends spr, scr, str, spl, squ

30. l Blends

Various consonants blend with l.

Blend		Examples		
bl	blue	blessing	blood	blister
cl	clip	clock	clothing	clatter
fl	flap	flower	flint	flash
gl	glass	glow	glitter	glen
pl	play	plow	plastic	plunge
sl	slam	slick	slender	slippery

30. l Blends

31. Sounds shr and thr

Sh and r and th and r form many words..

Examples

shr	shrapnel	shred	shrink	shrug	shriek
	shrine	shrub	shrill	shrimp	shrivel

thr	threat	trash	throne	thrown	thrifty
	through	three	throat	thrust	thread

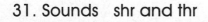

31. Sounds shr and thr

32. Sounds   nd, ng, nk, nt

Here are some words that end in two consonants. These words can be said by blending the letters together.

Blend	Examples			
nd	hand	stand	blend	find
ng	hang	sing	bring	riding
nk	ink	bank	hank	chunk
nt	ant	scent	haunt	different

32. Sounds   nd, ng, nk, nt

NOTES

NOTES

1. Prefixes

A <u>prefix</u> is an addition to the beginning of a word to form a related word. When adding a prefix, do not change the spelling of the prefix or the base word.

a + foot = afoot	mis + spell = misspell
dis + appear = disappear	over + stuffed = overstuffed
ex + patriot = ex-patriot	self + control = self-control
mid + night = midnight	un + tied = untied

When using **ex-** to mean former, always add a hyphen: ex-president.
When a word begins with **the same consonant** that a prefix ends with, keep both consonants: satisfied - dissatisfied.

1. Prefixes

2. Suffixes

A <u>suffix</u> is an addition to the end of a word to form a related word. When a word ends with the same consonant that the suffix begins with, keep both consonants: mean   meanness   real   really.

When adding a suffix that begins with a vowel to a one-syllable word that ends with a vowel and consonant, double the consonant before adding the suffix: sit   sitting   hop   hopping   slap   slapping.

When a two-syllable word ends with a vowel and a consonant and the word is accented on the last syllable, double the consonant before adding a suffix: begin   beginner   occur   occurrence.
Note: If the accent is shifted back from the last syllable when the suffix is added, the consonant is **not** doubled: refer   reference

2. Suffixes

3. Words ending in silent e

When a word ends in a consonant and silent **e**:
Keep the **e** when a suffix beginning with a consonant is added.

    care   careful   whole   wholeness   move   movement

Drop the **e** when adding a suffix beginning with a vowel.

    prove   provable   complete   completed   excite   exciting

When a word ends in a **ce** or **ge**, keep the e when adding a suffix that begins with **a** or **o** to preserve the soft sound (**c** like **s** or **z**, **g** like **j**).

    notice   noticeable   marriage   marriageable

When a word ends in ie, drop the e and change the i to a **y** before adding a suffix: die   dying   lie   lying   tie   tying

When a word ends in **ee**, keep the final **e** before any vowel except e:

    agree   agreeable   agreed   see   seeing   tree   treed

3. Words ending in silent e

4. Words ending in hard c and hard e

If the derived word will change the hard **c** to a soft **c**, do not add a **k** when adding the suffix.

electric	electricity
critic	criticize

When adding a suffix beginning with e, i, or y to a word ending with a hard **c**, add **k** before the suffix.

traffic   trafficked   trafficking

mimic   mimicked   mimicking   panic   panicky

Exceptions: comic, arc, talc, zinc

4. Words ending in hard c and hard e

5. Words ending in y

When a word ends in a consonant and a **y**, change the **y** to **i** when adding a suffix:

| busy | business | cry | cried |
| early | earlier | beauty | beautiful |

Exceptions to the **consonant** and **y** rule:

cry   crying   copy   copyist   pry   prying

When a word ends in a vowel and **y**, keep the **y** when adding a suffix.

pay   payable   employ   employable   employed

enjoy   enjoyable   enjoyment

Exceptions to the vowel rule:

| pay | paid | lay | laid |
| say | said | day | daily |

5. Words ending in y

6. The ie, ei rule

I before **e**,
except after **c**,
or when sounded like **a**
as in neighbor and sleigh.

i before **e**:   belief   piece   siege   shriek

e before **i** following **c**:   deceit   receive   ceiling   conceive

e before **i** when sounded like **a**:   weight   eight   vein

Some exceptions are: leisure   neither   weird   seize

6. The ie, ei rule

7. ly to form adverbs

The **ly** ending is generally used to form an adverb from an adjective, a participle, and, sometimes, a noun.

stern sternly	heat neatly	hopeful hopefully
critical critically	careless carelessly	mental mentally

When an adjective ends in **le**, the adverb is formed by changing the **e** to y.

simple simply	double doubly
able ably	responsible responsibly

When an adjective ends in **y**, form the adverb by changing the **y** to i before adding **ly**.

handy   handily   busy   busily   ready   readily

7. ly to form adverbs

8. Plural nouns rule

Most nouns add an **s** to form the plural.

> face faces bowl· bowls Paul Pauls cheese cheeses
> hour hours MacDonald MacDonalds

When a word ends in **ful**, the **s** to form the plural is added to the end of the word.

> handful handfuls capful capfuls shovelful shovelfuls
> spoonful spoonfuls

The plurals of proper nouns preceded by a title are formed by pluralizing either the title or the noun.

> Miss Brown or Misses Brown Dr. Hopkinses or Doctors Hopkins

8. Plural nouns rule

Add **es** to form the plural form for nouns that end in **ch**, **sh**, **ss**, **s**, **x**, **z**.

Ending	Examples:		
ch	church churches	bunch bunches	Blanch Blanches
sh	radish radishes	wish wishes	Bush Bushes
ss	business businesses	loss losses	Miss Misses
s	gas gases	bus buses	Jones Joneses
x	box boxes	tax taxes	fax faxes
z	adz adzes	Razz Razzes	Inez Inezes

Exceptions: some words ending in s or z double the ending consonant before adding **es**. yes yesses quiz quizzes

9. Plural nouns ending in ch, sh, ss, s, x, z

10. Plural nouns ending in y and o

When a word ends in a **consonant** and y or **qu** and y, change the y to **i** and add **es** to form the plural.

> fly flies soliloquy soliloquies berry berries

When a word ends in a **vowel** and y add **s** to form the plural.

> day days donkey donkeys

When a word ends in **o or oo**, add **s** or **es** to form the plural based on customary uses: radio radios zoo zoos

> portfolio portfolios tomato tomatoes
>
> potato potatoes buffalo buffaloes

NOTE: Technical music terms ending in o add only s.

> piano pianos solo solos soprano sopranos

10. Plural nouns ending in y and o

11. Plural nouns ending in f, fe, or ff

Most nouns ending in **f**, **fe**, or **ff** form the plural by adding an **s**.

cliff cliffs	if ifs	waif waifs
belief beliefs	chief chiefs	safe safes
proof proofs	roof roofs	surf surfs

Some nouns form the plural by changing the **f** to a **v** and adding **es**.

wife wives	half halves	thief thieves
knife knives	life lives	shelf shelves

The plural of some nouns ending in **f** or **ff** can be formed in more than one way. (The first spelling is preferred.)

scarf scarves or scarfs hoof hooves or hoofs

11. Plural nouns ending in f, fe, or ff

12. Plural compound nouns

To form the plural of a compound noun, use the final word.

bush bushes	rosebush rosebushes
shelf shelves	bookshelf bookshelves
cloth cloths	tablecloth tablecloths
ground grounds	playground playgrounds

To form the plural of a hyphenated noun, add **s or ies** to the main word only.

lady - in - waiting	ladies - in - waiting
father - in - law	fathers - in - law
bride - to - be	brides - to - be

12. Plural compound nouns

13. Plural forms of letters, signs, symbols, words

The plural of letters, signs, symbols and words functioning merely as words can be formed either by adding **s** or adding **'s**.

Use either form with uppercase letters and dates.

> Truman was president during the 1940's.
> Truman was president during the 1940s.
> All of the CPAs have licenses.
> All of the CPA's have licenses.

Use 's with lowercase letters, signs and words used as words.

> Dot your i's and cross your t's.
> Three !!!'s indicate strong emphasis.
> He used many no's in his refusal.
> Color the areas marked with 4's.

13. Plural forms of letters, signs, symbols, words

14. Plural forms of Latin and Greek nouns

Note: Many of these nouns have added a regular English plural as an acceptable alternative, as focus focuses.

Change the **us** in Latin words to **i**.

fungus fungi   alumnus alumni   focus foci

Change the **um** in Latin words to **a**.

curriculum curricula   addendum addenda

Change the **is** in Greek words to **es**.

oasis oases   analysis analyses   crisis crises

14. Plural forms of Latin and Greek nouns

15. Plural irregular nouns

Some nouns change their root spelling for the plural forms:
>   foot feet   mouse mice   tooth teeth
>   woman women   man men   goose geese

Some nouns have different plurals depending on their definitions.
>   die dies   (tools used to press patterns into materials)
>   die dice   (cubes marked with spots used in games)
>   fish fishes   (referring to a variety or kind)
>   fish fish   (referring to specific fish)

Some other irregular plural nouns are:
>   child children   deer deer   sheep sheep

15. Plural irregular nouns

16. Possessives

Possessive forms for most singular nouns are formed by adding an 's.
   telephone   telephone's   curtain   curtain's   Bill   Bill's
Plural nouns not ending in **s** add an 's.
   children   children's   men   men's   deer   deer's
Plural nouns ending in **s** add only the apostrophe.
   sisters   sisters'   hospitals   hospitals'   Stevens   Steven's
An 's added to the last noun of a compound subject will form the possessive.   Jim and Kevin's mother
An 's will show separate ownership.   Jim's and Kevin's report cards

The possessive form of a compound word is made with 's only after the last noun.   brother-in-law's car   brother-in-law's cars

16. Possessives

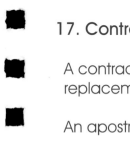

17. Contractions

A contraction is a shortened form of a word or word group by replacement of a letter or sound with an apostrophe.

An apostrophe can be used to replace a lost vowel.

do not don't   it is it's
we are we're   she is she's

An apostrophe can be used to replace the **ha** sound in have.

we have we"ve   you have you"ve

Irregular contractions: cannot can't   will not won't

17. **Contractions**

18. Compound words and numbers

Compound words are formed by combining two or more smaller words.

headline	nevertheless	halfhearted	anywhere
keyboard	anywhere	today	overcoat
outline	inasmuch	background	heartache

Hyphens are used with compound words if omission of the hyphen might cause confusion.

cell-like   great-grandmother   half-dollar

Hyphens are used in spelling compound numbers between twenty and one hundred and in fractions being used as adjectives or adverbs.

twenty-ninth   one thirty-third   fifty-first

18. Compound words and numbers

19. Suffixes tion sion

Write **tion** if a word ends in a vowel and the sound of **shun**.

Write **tion** if a word ends in any sound other than i, **n**, or **r**.
education   addition   action

Write **sion** if a word ends in a vowel and the sound of **zhun**.

Write **sion** if the word ends in an i.
vision   decision   propulsion   expulsion

Write **ssion** if the word ends in **ss**, **mit**, **ceed**, or **cede**.
discuss discussion omit omission
concede concession proceed procession

19. Suffixes tion sion

20. Suffixes able, ible

Write **able** when the base word can stand alone.
    fashionable comfortable laughable

Write **ible** when the base word cannot stand alone.
    possible responsible horrible

Write **ible** when the base word ends in **sion**, which will change to **ss**.
    admission admissible

Write **ible** to preserve the sound of a soft **c** or **g**.
    tangible intelligible legible invincible

20. Suffixes able, ible

When a noun ends in a consonant, do not change the spelling
before adding **ous**.

> danger   dangerous   humor   humorous

Exception: When a noun ends in f, change the f to v.

> grief   grievous   mischief   mischievous

When a noun ends in **e**, drop the **e** and add **ous**.

> adventure   adventurous   desire   desirous

Exception: Keep the **e** when you need to keep a soft **g** sound.

> courage   courageous   advantage   advantageous

When a noun ends in **y**, drop the **y** and add **e** before adding **ous**.

> beauty   beauteous   pity   piteous

21. Suffix ous

22. Suffixes ence, ense, ance

Write **ence**: when a noun is formed from a verb ending in **ere**;
when a noun has a soft **c** or **g** sound at the end;
when **cid**, **fid**, **sid**, **flu**, **gu**, or **sist** precede the ending.
interference coincidence confidence influence insistence

A few words end with **ense**: defense suspense immense expense
offense pretense

Write **ance** when the word has a hard **g** or **c** before the ending;
when the root word ends in **ate** or **ation**; and
when a noun is formed from a verb ending in **ear**, **ure** or **y**.
arrogance tolerance assurance

22. Suffixes ence, ense, ance

23. Suffixes ize, ise, yze

Write **ize** when adding to a word that can stand alone.

civil   civilize   mobile   mobilize
item   itemize   modern   modernize

Write **ise** when the last syllable of the word is not pronounced **iz**

promise   surprise   disguise

or when the **ise** is part of the word itself (not a suffix).

televise   excise   merchandise

The **yze** ending is the least common. Here are two examples.

analyze   paralyze

23. Suffixes ize, ise, yze

24. Suffixes cede, ceed, sede

The endings **cede**, **ceed**, and **sede** all sound like the word **seed**.

The commonly used ending for this sound is **cede**.
Example: precede   accede   intercede
          concede   recede   secede

A few words end in **ceed**.
Example: exceed   proceed   succeed

Only one common word ends in **sede**.
Example: supersede

24. Suffixes cede, ceed, sede

25. Suffixes efy, ify

The endings **efy** and **ify** sound like the words "**if I**" said together.

The most commonly used ending is **ify**.
Examples: fortify dignify magnify falsify   beautify
notify gratify glorify clarify identify

Only four common words use the **efy** ending.
Examples: liquefy   putrefy   rarefy   stupefy

25. Suffixes efy, ify

26. Suffixes ious, eous

The endings **ious** and **eous** sound like the sounds "e us" said together.

Most words ending with this sound use the **ious** spelling.

Examples:
delicious	ambitious	glorious
cautious	tedious	various
anxious	licentious	infectious

Many technical or scientific words use the **eous** spelling.

Examples:
erroneous	nauseous	heterogeneous
extraneous	courteous	herbaceous

27. Suffixes al, el, le

No rule exists for using the **al, el, le** endings. The **le** ending is used more frequently than **al** or **el**.

Common words ending in **al**.
Examples: personal   fiscal   proposal   refusal   electrical

Common words ending in **el**.
Examples: bushel   travel   nickel   parcel

Common words ending in **le**.
Examples: double   people   shuttle   chuckle   example
              principle

27. Suffixes al, el, le

28. Suffixes er, or, ar

Both **er** and **or** mean one who or that which. No rule exists for determining **er** and **or** endings. The **or** ending is more common.

Common **or** words: actor, administrator, author, coordinator, governor, inventor, operator, sponsor, bachelor, collector, educator, radiator

Common **er** words: advertiser, manager, passenger, employer, officer, laborer, consumer, interpreter

A few words end in **ar**: dollar, beggar, grammar, familiar, collar, regular, peculiar, liar

28. Suffixes er, or, ar

29. Suffixes ery, ary, ory

Over 300 words end in **ary**.

Examples: supplementary   secretary   complimentary

Most words ending in **ery** are nouns.

Examples: cemetery   stationery   tomfoolery

Exceptions: Adjectives formed by adding **y** to a noun.

blustery   splintery   summery

If you can add the **ion** ending and form a word, the correct spelling is probably **ory**.

Examples: direct   direction   directory
transit   transition   transitory

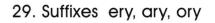

29. Suffixes ery, ary, ory

30. Often Misspelled Words

absence	amateur	believe	complement
accidentally	analyze	benefit	compliment
accuracy	annually	breathe	conscience
acknowledgment	anticipated	bureaucracy	convenient
acquaintance	appearance	business	courtesy
acquire	assassination	calendar	criticized
actually	athletic	career	curiosity
adapt	attendance	catalog	decide
adolescent	author	category	description
affect	auxiliary	certain	diagnosis
alright	awkward	character	disappear
although	beginning	choose	disease
amateur	belief	committee	dividend

30. Often Misspelled Words

division	familiar	individual	maintain
efficient	favorite	intelligent	maintenance
envelope	financially	interest	meant
environment	forty	invariably	minutes
equipment	government	irresistible	mortgage
escape	governor	jewelry	mountain
especially	guarantee	knowledgeable	negotiate
excellent	height	label	ninety
except	horizontal	laboratory	noticeable
exercise	humorous	leisurely	nuclear
experience	imaginary	license	occurrence
explanation	immediately	literature	occurring
facsimile	independent	magnificent	opportunity

32. Often Misspelled Words

parameter	procedure	scarcity	superintendent
particle	professor	schedule	technicality
particularly	pronunciation	secretary	tension
peculiar	proposal	separate	thorough
performance	psychology	signature	through
permanent	received	significant	twelfth
pleasant	recommend	society	unfortunate
possible	religious	someone	until
practically	remember	stationary	vitamin
precede	restaurant	stationery	weird
preference	reversible	statistics	writing
prescription	sacrifice	strategy	xylophone
privilege	satellite	suburban	yield

32. Often Misspelled Words

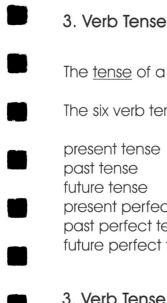

3. Verb Tense

The <u>tense</u> of a verb refers to the <u>time</u> of the action or state of being.

The six verb tenses:

present tense	I walk, he walks
past tense	I walked, he walked
future tense	I shall walk, he shall walk, I will walk, he will walk
present perfect tense	I have walked, he has walked
past perfect tense	I had walked, he had walked
future perfect tense	I shall have walked, he shall have walked

3. Verb Tense

4. Infinitive and Past Participle Verb Forms

<u>Definitions:</u>
<u>Infinitive</u> form is the word **to** followed by the verb. (to run)
<u>Past participle</u> form indicates a completed action. (walk, have walked, shall have walked)
<u>Regular verbs</u>: To form the past tense and past participle forms, add **d** or **ed** to the present tense or infinitive.
<u>Irregular verbs</u> do not follow this rule.

Examples:	present tense	infinitive	past tense	past participle
Regular	walk	to walk	walked	(have) walked
Irregular	run	to run	ran	(have) run

4. Infinitive and Past Participle Verb Forms